Rebirth
OF A People

Sean Price

Raintree
Chicago, Illinois

© 2007 Raintree
Published by Raintree,
an imprint of Capstone Global Library, LLC
Chicago, Illinois

Customer Service 888-363-4266

Visit our website at www.heinemannraintree.com

All rights reserved. No part of this publication may be reproduced or transmitted in any form or by any means, electronic or mechanical, including photocopying, recording, taping, or any information storage and retrieval system, without permission in writing from the publisher.

Designed by Michelle Lisseter, Kim Miracle, and Bigtop
Printed and bound in the United States of America, North Mankato, MN

13 12 11
10 9 8 7 6 5 4 3 2

Library of Congress Cataloging-in-Publication Data
Price, Sean.
  Rebirth of a people : Harlem Renaissance / Sean Price.
      p. cm. -- (American history through primary sources)
  Includes bibliographical references and index.
  ISBN 1-4109-2415-7 (hc) -- ISBN 1-4109-2426-2 (pb)
  1. African Americans--Intellectual life--20th century--Juvenile literature. 2. Harlem Renaissance--Juvenile literature--Juvenile literature. 3. African American arts--20th century--Juvenile literature. 4. Harlem (New York, N.Y.)--Intellectual life--20th century--Juvenile literature. 5. African Americans--New York (State)--New York--Intellectual life--20th century--Juvenile literature. 6. African American arts--New York (State)--New York--History--20th century--Juvenile literature. 7. New York (N.Y.)--Intellectual life--20th century--Juvenile literature. I. Title. II. Series.

E185.6.P83 2006
974.7'1--dc22

2006008486

13-digit ISBNs
978-1-4109-2415-5 (hardcover)
978-1-4109-2426-1 (paperback)

062011
006158RP

Acknowledgments
The author and publisher are grateful to the following for permission to reproduce copyright material: Corbis **pp. 4–5**, **6** (Bettmann), **7** (Lucien Aigner), **8** (Hulton-Deutsch Collection), **9** (Bettmann), **11** (Underwood & Underwood), **14** (left), **15** (Underwood & Underwood), **18** (John Springer Collection), **22**, **24** (Christie's Images), **29** (Bettmann); Getty Images **p. 17**; The Granger Collection **pp. 25**, **27**; The Harlem Globetrotters **p. 13**; James VanDerZee (Donna Mussenden VanDerZee) **p. 12**; Library of Congress Prints and Photographs Division **p. 21**; The New York Public Library, Astor and Lennox Tilden Foundations (Manuscripts Archives and Rare Books Division, Schomburg Center for Research in Black Culture) **pp. 14** (right), **19**.

Cover photograph of "Jitterbug" dancers in Harlem in the 1930s reproduced with permission of Corbis/Bettmann.

Photo research by Tracy Cummins.

Illustrations by Darren Lingard.

The publishers would like to thank Nancy Harris and Joy Rogers for their assistance in the preparation of this book.

Every effort has been made to contact copyright holders of any material reproduced in this book. Any omissions will be rectified in subsequent printings if notice is given to the publishers.

Disclaimer
All the Internet addresses (URLs) given in this book were valid at the time of going to press. However, due to the dynamic nature of the Internet, some addresses may have changed, or sites may have changed or ceased to exist since publication. While the author and publishers regret any inconvenience this may cause readers, no responsibility for any such changes can be accepted by either the author or the publishers.

It is recommended that adults supervise children on the Internet.

Contents

Rebirth of a People	4
Harlem's Golden Age	6
A Place to Party	8
Churchgoin'	10
Rens and Globetrotters	12
Powerful Voices	14
The Jazz Age	16
Wowing the Crowd	18
Women of Harlem	20
"I, Too"	22
The Picture Takin' Man	24
Changing Times	26
Dancing in Harlem	28
Glossary	30
Want to Know More?	31
Index	32

Some words are printed in bold, **like this**. You can find out what they mean on page 30. You can also look in the box at the bottom of the page where they first appear.

Rebirth of a People

Harlem is a neighborhood in New York City. In 1900 blacks began moving to Harlem. During this period, blacks did not have the same rights as whites in the United States. They could not live or work in the same places. They could not eat in the same places.

Blacks moved to Harlem because it offered them better housing. By 1920 this small neighborhood was filled mostly with black people.

Many talented people lived in Harlem. Writers, painters, and other artists lived there. They wrote about black history. They created new songs and paintings. Others became famous actors. Together, they created the Harlem Renaissance.

Thousands of blacks ▶ moved to Harlem in the early 1900s.

renaissance rebirth or revival

Renaissance is a French word. It means "rebirth" or "revival." The Harlem Renaissance was a chance to start over for black Americans. They had the chance to make a better life in an all-black neighborhood. Whites could not tell them how to behave. Black Americans could finally show what they could do.

Harlem's Golden Age

Blacks enjoyed life in Harlem. They enjoyed shopping. They also liked going to restaurants and clubs.

People worked hard. Many men were **porters**. Porters are bag carriers on trains or at hotels. Others worked as doormen and janitors. Some worked as bricklayers. Women worked as house cleaners, nurses, or beauticians.

Harlem was famous for its fun nightlife. ▼

Most people in Harlem crowded into small apartments. People who live in apartments pay rent to a landlord. Harlem apartments cost a lot. Harlem families paid higher rent than other New Yorkers. Rent took up almost half of the money a family earned. Landlords knew that blacks would pay it. They wanted to live in Harlem.

▲ *Eating out was a treat for Harlem residents.*

porter   bag carrier

A Place to Party

Many Harlem families could not pay their rent. Sometimes the cost of other bills went up, too. Many people did not have enough money.

"Rent parties" helped people in Harlem make ends meet. The host (person giving the party) charged friends and neighbors **admission**. Admission is an entry fee. Usually it was no more than 25 cents. Money raised at rent parties helped people pay the rent.

▼ *Apartments in Harlem were expensive. But people wanted to be close to friends and family.*

admission	entry fee
amateur	person who does something part-time or as a hobby; not a professional

These parties helped people meet neighbors and enjoy life in Harlem. **Amateur** (part-time) musicians kept people dancing. They danced the Charleston. This was one of the most popular dance steps of the 1920s.

People looked forward to celebrating big events.

Churchgoin'

There was a church on almost every block in Harlem. Some ministers (church leaders) turned stores into churches. Other ministers wandered the streets. They would give **sermons**. Sermons are religious speeches. Ministers also held religious meetings. They were called **revivals**. Revivals might be held right on the sidewalk.

Harlem had many large churches. The biggest was the Abyssinian Baptist Church. Its pastor was Adam Clayton Powell Sr. He was a strong leader. Powell turned the church into a help center for the poor. It was also a help center for the **uneducated**. Uneducated people have spent little or no time in school.

*"I want to establish the kingdom of **social justice**,"* Powell said.

Social justice meant giving help to those who needed it. Homeless people could get meals. Church members taught people how to read and do math. They showed poor people how to get jobs, such as dressmaking.

revival	religious meeting
sermon	religious speech
social justice	helping the poor and uneducated
uneducated	someone who has spent little or no time in school

◀ Adam Clayton Powell Sr. urged his congregation to help the poor.

Rens and Globetrotters

Harlem had a strong professional basketball team. A group of Harlem players started a team called the New York **Renaissance.** This was in 1922. People called them the Rens for short. Some white teams refused to play the Rens. But the Rens won their first world championship in 1939.

The Rens were a great success. They won 2,588 games and lost only 529. The team broke up in 1949.

The Rens' success paved the way for a better-known team. It is called the Harlem Globetrotters. The Globetrotters got started in Chicago in 1927. Even so, the Globetrotters' owner put "Harlem" in the team name. He wanted people to know its players were black.

The Globetrotters began clowning around when they played. Fans liked their jokes more than serious basketball. The Globetrotters started doing trick shots. This excited crowds. Their fancy ball handling made other teams look foolish. The team became famous for its dazzling moves.

▼ The first Harlem Globetrotters were really from Chicago.

Powerful Voices

DuBois

W. E. B. DuBois was a well-known black **scholar**. A scholar is a very educated person. He wrote a famous book called *The Souls of Black Folk*. DuBois also worked in Harlem at *The Crisis*. This was a magazine. It was for the National Association for the Advancement of **Colored** People (NAACP). Colored was a common word for blacks then. The NAACP fought to help blacks. Many Americans read *The Crisis*.

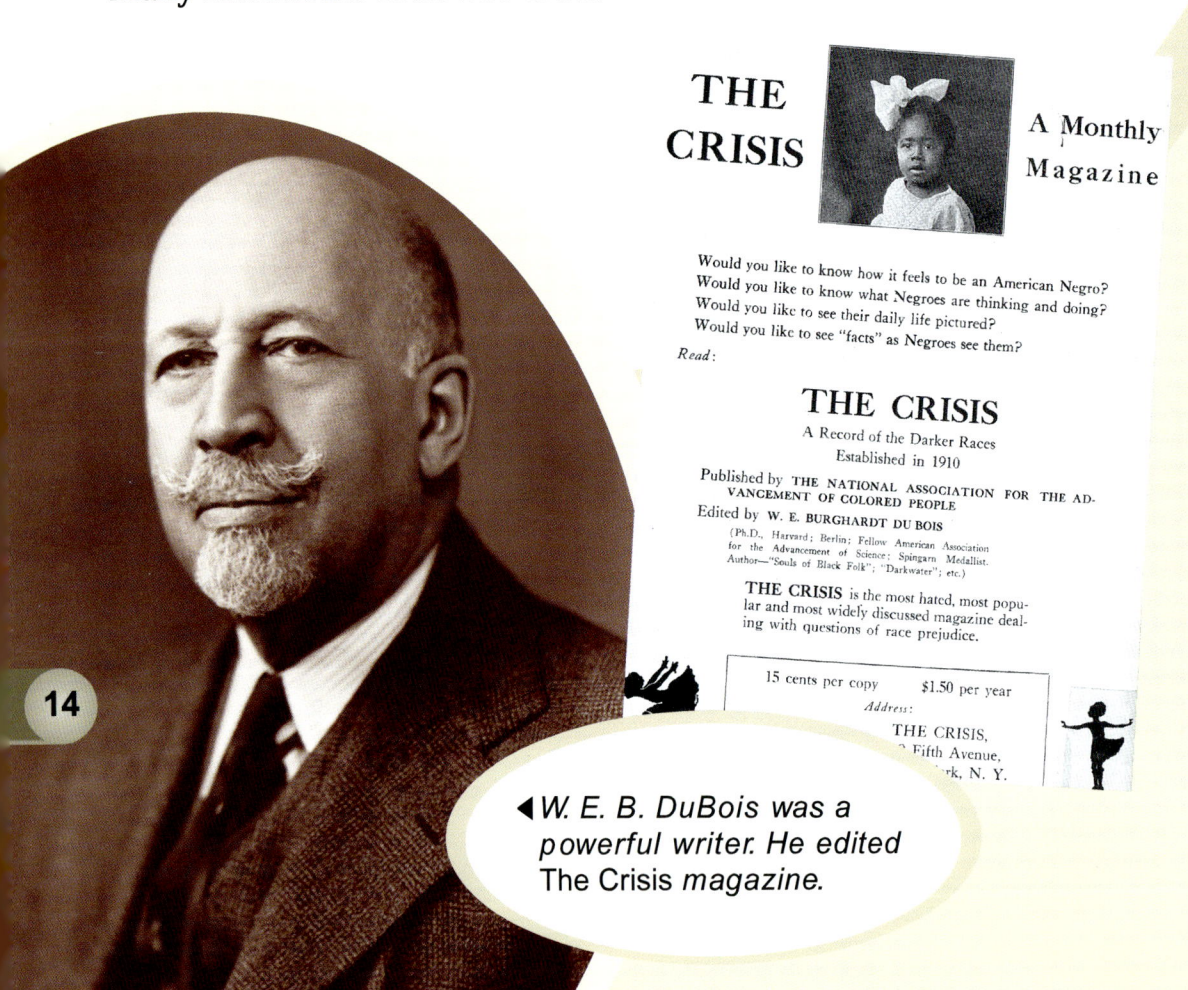

◀ W. E. B. DuBois was a powerful writer. He edited The Crisis *magazine*.

Marcus Garvey had ▶
many followers across
the United States.

Garvey

Marcus Garvey was another powerful person in Harlem. He believed that blacks should create their own jobs. He believed they should create their own businesses. Garvey even created his own army. Garvey ran a newspaper called **Negro** World. Negro was another common word for blacks at the time. It had more readers than any other black newspaper. Garvey was a very popular leader in Harlem.

colored	common word for blacks during the 1920s
Negro	common word for blacks during the 1920s
scholar	very educated person

The Jazz Age

During the Harlem **Renaissance**, many new types of art formed. Black writers and singers started new styles. So did black actors. They wanted to say new things.

Many people in Harlem liked a type of southern music. It was called the blues. Blues singers sang sweet, sad songs. These songs were about the problems of regular people.

Perhaps the biggest art form of the time was jazz. In fact, the 1920s are called the Jazz Age. The people of Harlem loved jazz. It was brand new. Two famous jazz artists were Louis Armstrong and Duke Ellington. Armstrong played the trumpet. Ellington was a bandleader.

Musicians played jazz at many nightspots. The Cotton Club and Savoy Ballroom were two of the biggest. Black artists could perform at the Cotton Club. But they could not go there as guests. The Savoy Ballroom was different. The Savoy allowed blacks to perform. They could also go there to dance.

▼ *Duke Ellington became Harlem's most popular bandleader.*

Wowing the Crowd

Many black actors performed in Harlem. Some also lived in Harlem. Two very famous performers were Josephine Baker and Paul Robeson.

Josephine Baker worked as a dancer at Harlem nightclubs. Baker made people notice her by rolling her eyes. She also pretended to be clumsy. Audiences howled with laughter. Baker was a big hit in Harlem. She was a superstar at the age of twenty. The year was 1926.

◀ *Josephine Baker's humor made her a star.*

Paul Robeson was the best-known black actor of his time.

Paul Robeson was first a football player. He also worked as a lawyer. Robeson had a deep, beautiful voice. It was perfect for the stage. He started acting. Robeson performed in many plays. He later appeared in movies. His best-known movie is *Showboat*. It was filmed in 1936.

Women of Harlem

Black writers in Harlem wrote books. They wrote plays and other works.

At first, few could get their work **published** (printed). That changed during the Harlem **Renaissance.**

Zora Neale Hurston was a talented Harlem writer. She wrote about the problems faced by blacks. She wanted to keep those problems from controlling her life. In "How It Feels to be **Colored** Me," she wrote:

*Someone is always at my elbow reminding me that I am a granddaughter of **slaves**. It fails to register depression with me [to make me sad].*

publish to print or bring to the public's attention
slave person owned by another person

A'Lelia Walker was a millionaire. She helped young writers. She helped Zora Neale Hurston. Walker had a townhouse in Harlem. It was called the Dark Tower. It became the top meeting place for black writers.

▼ *Writers like Zora Neale Hurston helped spread Harlem's fame.*

"I, Too"

Langston Hughes was a famous Harlem poet. He wrote in a free and open way. His poems were easy to read. Hughes also wrote plays and books. But he is most famous for his poems. Poems like "I, Too" showed how black people struggled. Many people in Harlem worked as servants. They were butlers and maids. They could not walk in the front door of a white person's house. They could not eat at a white person's table.

Langston Hughes ▶ wrote many powerful poems about black life.

"I, Too"

I, too, sing America.

I am the darker brother.

They send me to eat in the kitchen

When company comes,

But I laugh,

And eat well,

And grow strong.

Tomorrow,

I'll be at the table

When company comes.

Nobody'll dare

Say to me,

"Eat in the kitchen,"

Then.

Besides,

They'll see how beautiful I am

And be ashamed—

I, too, am America.

The Picture Takin' Man

James Van Der Zee was known as the "picture takin' man." People asked him to take photos. He took pictures at weddings, birthdays, and many other places.

Many outsiders saw Harlem as a run-down neighborhood. But Van Der Zee's photographs show something different. His pictures show wealthy homes. They show men wearing service medals. They show men getting their weekly haircuts. They show little girls learning to dance.

Van Der Zee's photos▶ showed that Harlem was not just a poor neighborhood.

By the 1960s, Van Der Zee's photos became popular outside of Harlem. People saw that they recorded black history. The pictures showed some of the forgotten people of the Harlem **Renaissance.**

Strivers' Row

Rich people lived in Harlem, too. Harlem's well-to-do lawyers and doctors lived on "Strivers' Row." A striver is someone who tries to do better. The very rich lived on a block called Sugar Hill.

▼ Photographer James Van Der Zee captured Harlem's daily activities.

Changing Times

Archibald Motley Jr. was a painter. He did not live in Harlem. But he was one of the first painters to focus on black life. His paintings showed Harlem's spirit. People believed in Harlem's new energy. They believed in Harlem's art and business. Some people felt that Harlem art and business could help blacks all over the United States.

But in 1929, the **Great Depression** began. Jobs became hard to find for everyone. Even before the Depression, many blacks had a tough time getting jobs. About half of Harlem's workers had no jobs during the Depression.

That meant people in Harlem had little money. They could not buy art and books. So, Harlem's artists and writers left. They found other work. The Harlem Renaissance came to an end in the late 1930s. Still, Harlem remained an important place for blacks. The Harlem Renaissance created pride and hope. These feelings never went away.

Great Depression   period when many Americans could not find jobs

▼ This painting by Archibald Motley Jr. shows people enjoying life in Harlem.

Dancing in Harlem

The 1920s had many **fads**. A fad is something that is popular for a brief time. Dancing the Charleston became a huge fad. Southern blacks brought it to Harlem. That helped spread it across the United States.

The Charleston gave Harlem dancer "Shorty" George Snowden an idea. He used the Charleston to create another big dance. The new dance was called the Lindy Hop. The Lindy Hop was like the Charleston. People swung their arms and kicked their feet. But the Lindy Hop let people move more freely.

The Lindy Hop led to other new dances. Perhaps the biggest was the Jitterbug. It became popular in the 1930s and 1940s. All of these dances were performed to jazz music. At the time, it was the most popular music among young people.

fad something popular for a brief time

▼ Popular dances like the Lindy Hop and the Jitterbug got their start in Harlem.

Glossary

admission entry fee

amateur person who does something part-time or as a hobby; not a professional

colored common word for blacks during the first half of the 1900s

fad something popular for a brief time

Great Depression period when many Americans could not find jobs. It lasted from 1929 to 1941.

Negro common word for blacks during the first half of the 1900s

porter bag carrier

publish to print or bring to the public's attention

renaissance rebirth or revival

revival religious meeting

scholar very educated person

sermon religious speech

slave person owned by another person

social justice helping the poor and uneducated

uneducated someone who has spent little or no time in school

Want to Know More?

Books to read

- Jordan, Denise. *Harlem Renaissance Artists*. Chicago: Heinemann Library, 2003.
- Raatma, Lucia. *The Harlem Renaissance. A Celebration of Creativity*. Chanhassen, Minn.: Child's World, 2003.

Websites

- http://artsedge.kennedy-center.org/exploring/harlem/artsedge.html

  Visit *Drop Me Off in Harlem: Exploring the Intersections* to learn more about the artists, musicians, and writers of the Harlem Renaissance.

- http://www.si.umich.edu/chico/Harlem

  Explore *Harlem 1900-1940: An African-American Community* to learn more about the history of Harlem.

Read **Counting Coup: Customs of the Crow Nation** to find out about the history and traditions of the Crow people.

To find out about the struggle against segregation read **When Will I Get In?: Segregation and Civil Rights**.

Index

actors 16, 18
admission 8
amateurs 8, 9
Armstrong, Louis 16
artists 16, 26, 27

Baker, Josephine 18, 19
blues 16

Charleston (dance) 9, 28
churches 10–11

dances 9, 28–29
Dark Tower 21
DuBois, W.E.B. 14
education 10
Ellington, Duke 16, 17

fads 28

Garvey, Marcus 15
Great Depression 26

Harlem 4, 6–7, 14, 15, 18, 24, 25, 26
Harlem Globetrotters 12–13
Hughes, Langston 22–23
Hurston, Zora Neale 20, 21

jazz 16, 28
Lindy Hop 28, 29
Motley, Jr., Archibald 26, 27
musicians 16–17

negroes 15
New York Rens 12, 13

porters 6
Powell, Sr., Adam Clayton 10, 11
publishing 20

renaissance 4, 5
rent parties 8–9
revivals 10
Robeson, Paul 18

scholars 14
sermons 10
Snowden, George "Shorty" 28
social justice 10
strivers 25

Van der Zee, James 24–25

Walker, A'Lelia 21
writers 16, 20–23, 26